Fast, Faster, Fastest

By Miriam Frost
Illustrated by John Emil Cymerman

Running is fast,

2

but roller skates are faster.

3

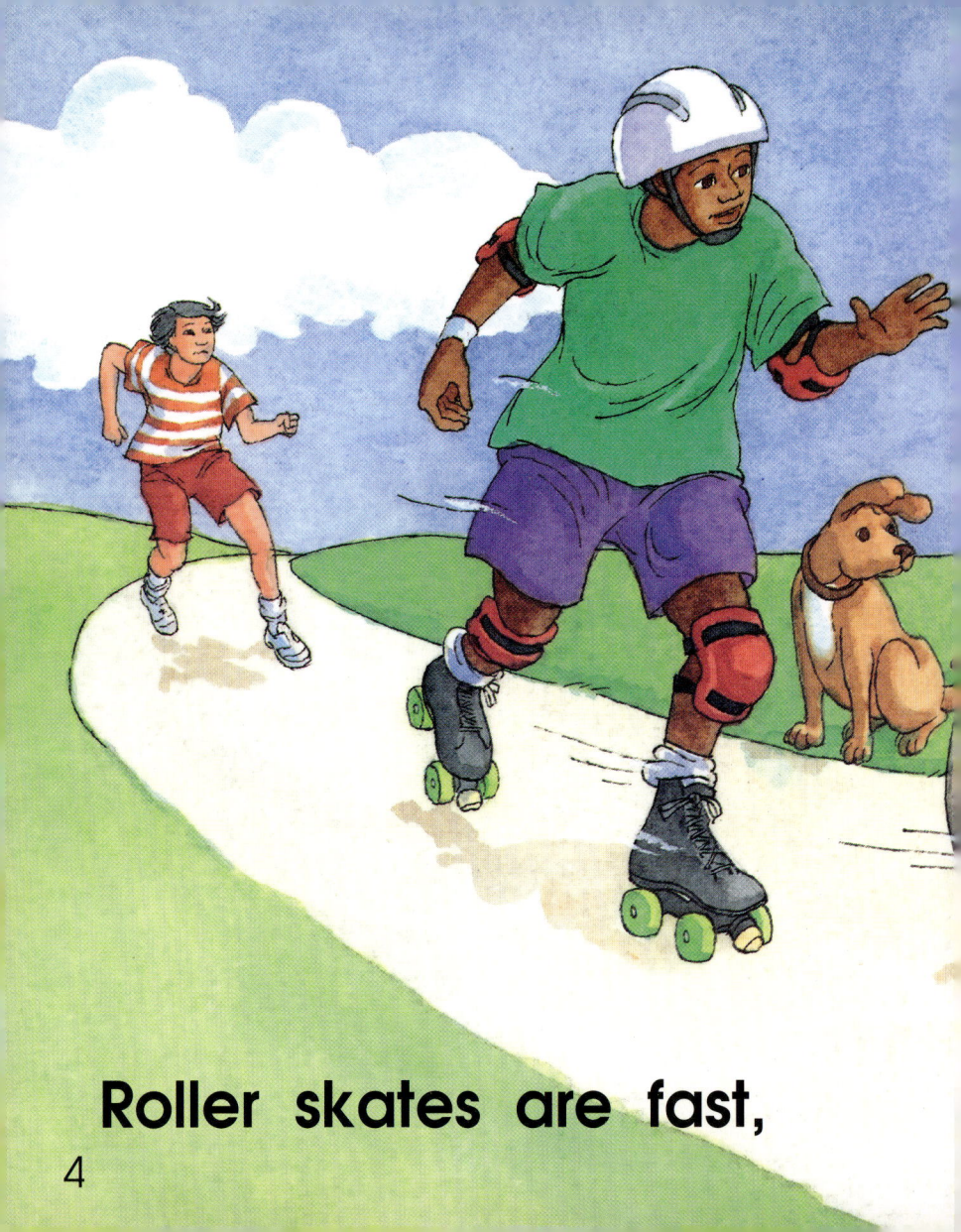

Roller skates are fast,

4

but a bike is faster.

A bike is fast,

but a motorbike is faster.

A motorbike is fast,

but a taxi is faster.

A taxi is fast,

but a train is faster.

A train is fast,

but a plane is faster.

13

A plane is fast,

14

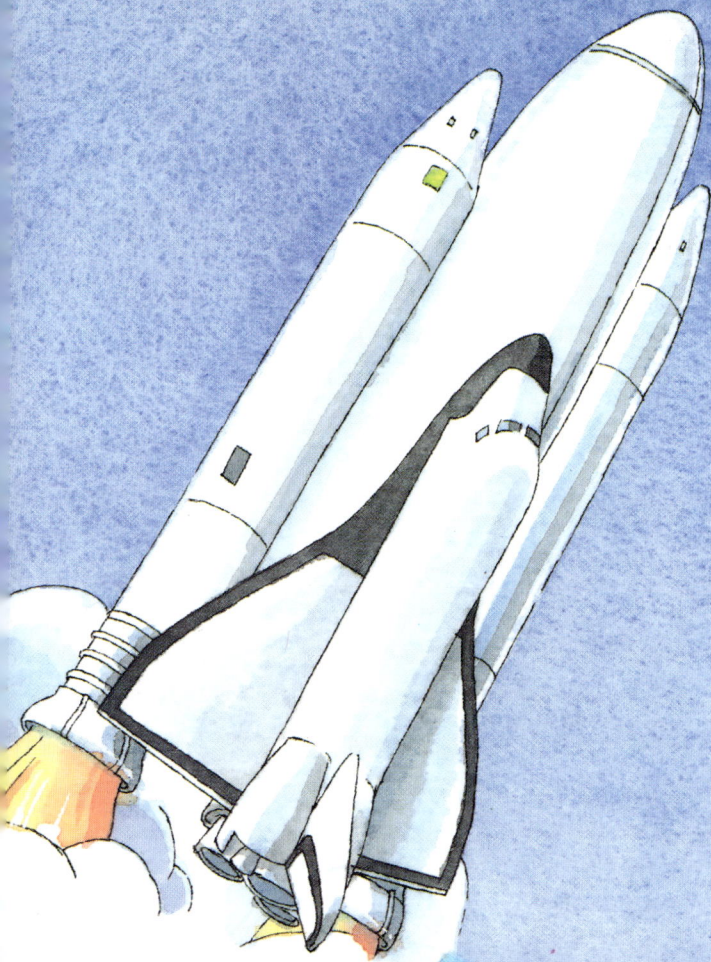

but a space shuttle is...

15

the fastest of all!

16